DRAMA CLAS

The Drama Classics
greatest plays in affordable paperback editions for students,
actors and theatregoers. The hallmarks of the series are
accessible introductions, uncluttered texts and an overall
theatrical perspective.

Given that readers may be encountering a particular play
for the first time, the introduction seeks to fill in the
theatrical/historical background and to outline the chief
themes rather than concentrate on interpretational and
textual analysis. Similarly the play-texts themselves are free
of footnotes and other interpolations: instead there is an
end-glossary of 'difficult' words and phrases.

The texts of the English-language plays in the series
have been prepared taking full account of all existing
scholarship. The foreign-language plays have been newly
translated into a modern English that is both actable and
accurate: many of the translators regularly have their work
staged professionally.

Edited until his early death by Kenneth McLeish, the
Drama Classics series continues with his aim of providing
a first-class library of dramatic literature representing the
best of world theatre.

Associate editors:
Professor Trevor R. Griffiths
Dr. Colin Counsell
School of Arts and Humanities
University of North London

DRAMA CLASSICS *the first hundred*

*The publishers welcome
suggestions for further titles*

DRAMA CLASSICS

'TIS PITY SHE'S A WHORE

by

John Ford

edited and introduced by
Lisa Hopkins

NICK HERN BOOKS

London

www.nickhernbooks.co.uk

A Drama Classic

This edition of *'Tis Pity She's a Whore* first published
in Great Britain as a paperback original in 2003
by Nick Hern Books, 14 Larden Road, London W3 7ST

Copyright in the introduction © 2003 Nick Hern Books

Copyright in this edition of the text © 2003 Lisa Hopkins

Typeset by Country Setting, Kingsdown, Kent CT14 8ES
Printed by Bookmarque, Croydon, Surrey

A CIP catalogue record for this book is available from
the British Library

ISBN 1 85459 169 X

Introduction

John Ford (1586-?)

Infuriatingly little is known about Ford's life. He was born in Ilsington, Devon, in 1586, and went first to Exeter College, Oxford and then, like many other young Elizabethan men of good family, to study law at the Middle Temple in London, one of the Inns of Court. Unusually, he seems to have stayed there for the rest of his life, though he was never called to the bar. Since he was a younger son rather than the heir, he would have had to earn his living somehow, and it is usually thought that he must have done some kind of legal work. Some phrases in the dedication of *'Tis Pity She's a Whore* suggest that he may also have travelled abroad, probably in the mid 1620s. He never married, and although his early poetry refers to his love for a woman called Lycia, this is clearly a made-up name, so perhaps the woman herself was equally fictitious.

Although he published a few poems and prose works as a young man, Ford did not start writing plays until late in life, first in collaboration with other, established playwrights such as Dekker, Rowley, and Webster, and finally on his own. *'Tis Pity She's a Whore*, which he refers to in the dedication as 'these first fruits of my leisure', was published in 1633; we do not know when it was first written and performed, but some time in the later 1620s seems the likeliest, making Ford at least forty years old. He went on to write six more plays. Three were tragedies, like *'Tis Pity*; one revived the long defunct form of the chronicle history play; and the final two were tragicomedies, though comedy was never Ford's forte and both contain some very weak scenes. After the publication of his last known play, *The Lady's Trial*, in 1638, nothing further is heard of him.

The writer Gerard Langbaine, writing not long after the last known mention of Ford, declared that he had been friendly with all the major literary figures of the age. The only other contemporary hint about him comes from Heminges' *Elegy on Randolph's Finger*, where we find the couplet 'Deep in a dump Jack Ford alone was gat / With folded arms and melancholy hat', and this would certainly tie in with the dark tone of his work and his deep interest in troubled personalities and disordered mental states.

'Tis Pity She's a Whore: **What Happens in the Play**

The play is set in the Italian city of Parma. Giovanni, the hero, has just returned home from university at Bologna, accompanied by his tutor, Friar Bonaventura. During the opening conversation, Giovanni reveals to the friar that he is in love with his own sister, Annabella. The friar is horrified and tells him he must conquer his passion. In the next scene, we are introduced to some of the other suitors for Annabella's hand, Grimaldi, a Roman nobleman, and Soranzo, an important local gentleman, who are bitter rivals; we also meet Florio, father of Giovanni and Annabella. Finally, we meet Annabella herself, and her companion, the ominously-named Putana (it is Italian for 'whore'), who, in one of the play's many parallels with *Romeo and Juliet*, are standing on the balcony, the upper stage space. Putana wants to know which of her suitors Annabella prefers, and points out another of them, the idiotic Bergetto, who enters briefly with his rather wiser servant Poggio; Annabella, however, shows no interest in any man until Giovanni appears below. At first she appears not to recognise him (perhaps because he has been away at university) and asks who this handsome but unhappy-looking man can be; then, when Putana points out that it is Giovanni, Annabella joins him − symbolically going down from the balcony as a sign that she is about to make a moral as well as a literal descent − and asks him what is the matter. Giovanni confesses his love and Annabella replies that she loves him just as much. Having sworn fidelity to each other, they exit to consummate the relationship. Florio meanwhile is still occupied with the question of Annabella's marriage, and although we know that he has already promised her to Soranzo, he is also negotiating with Donado, uncle of the foolish Bergetto.

Act Two begins with Giovanni and Annabella emerging from the bedroom, teasing each other about what they have done. Giovanni takes his leave. Putana comes on and expresses no disapproval of the incest, but then Florio arrives with a new visitor: a supposed doctor called Richardetto, and his niece Philotis. Richardetto, we soon learn, is the husband of Hippolita, a woman who was seduced by Annabella's prospective husband Soranzo; he is so ashamed by this that he has disguised himself and let it be supposed that he is dead. Indeed we meet Hippolita in the next scene, angrily confronting Soranzo about his desertion of her and his proposed marriage to Annabella. She is eventually calmed by Soranzo's servant Vasques, who pretends to go along with her plans for revenge on Soranzo. We then see Richardetto reveal his true identity in conversation with Philotis and, in pursuance of his own plan to be revenged on Soranzo, warn Grimaldi that it is Soranzo who is Florio's preferred suitor for his daughter. He offers to poison Grimaldi's rapier so that he can kill

Soranzo. Meanwhile Bergetto meets Philotis after a brawl in the street and decides that he much prefers her to Annabella; Giovanni confesses to the horrified friar that he has slept with his sister; and Florio tells Annabella that he intends her to marry Soranzo.

Act Three sees Soranzo's first attempt to court Annabella, secretly observed by the jealous Giovanni. She rebuffs him, but then she faints; Putana reveals to Giovanni that she is pregnant. Florio consults Richardetto and Giovanni consults the friar, who both advise immediate marriage, and the friar terrifies Annabella into agreeing by warning her that otherwise she will go to hell. Meanwhile Bergetto and Philotis have sneaked away to be married, but Bergetto is killed by Grimaldi, who, in the darkness, mistakes him for Soranzo. Grimaldi is shielded by his relative the Cardinal.

Act Four begins just after the wedding of Annabella and Soranzo. Hippolita arrives diguised and tries to poison Soranzo, but is prevented by Vasques, who tricks her into drinking the poison herself. Appalled by everything that has happened, Richardetto advises Philotis to become a nun; she agrees and is not seen again. Soranzo discovers Annabella's pregnancy, but, though he threatens her, she will not reveal who the father is; however, Vasques tricks it out of Putana, and then gets his hired banditti to blind and imprison her.

Act Five opens with Annabella repentant, standing once more on the balcony from which she had descended into incest. She is found by the friar, who blesses her and agrees to take a letter to Giovanni urging him to repent. Soranzo, planning revenge, invites Giovanni and Florio to celebrate his birthday, and a defiant Giovanni agrees. On arriving at Soranzo's house, Giovanni goes first to see Annabella, and kills her. He then appears at the birthday feast with her heart

impaled on his dagger. Florio drops dead. Soranzo calls for
his banditti, but Giovanni manages to kill him, before being
himself finished off by Vasques. The Cardinal is left to pass
judgement on those who survive; he banishes Vasques and
confiscates all the money and property of the deceased.

The Title

John Ford took trouble with the publication of his plays,
procuring commendatory verses from his friends and
devising an anagram (*Fide honor*, honour through faith) of
Iohn Forde, one form of his name, to go on the title-pages
of the later ones (though not of this). Probably as a result,
'Tis Pity She's a Whore is unusually free of errors or textual
difficulties for a Renaissance play. There is, however, one
notorious ambiguity. Towards the close of the play, the
Cardinal orders,

> Peace!-First this woman, chief in these effects:
> My sentence is, that forthwith she be ta'en
> Out of the city, for example's sake,
> There to be burnt to ashes.

When he says 'this woman, chief in these effects', the
Cardinal must be talking either about the dead body of
Annabella or about Putana. In either case, his sentence may
well appear unnecessarily vindictive. Annabella has already
been stabbed and butchered, and Putana has been blinded –
the traditional punishment for incest, as in Sophocles'
Oedipus Rex. Surely both have suffered enough.

We may, moreover, question what right the Cardinal has to
pass sentence at all. As in so many of the plays of Protestant
Renaissance England, it has already been made quite
obvious that the Catholic church is venal and corrupt, and

that the opinions of its highest officers are for sale. While the Friar has struggled, however unsuccessfully, to do his best by all concerned and to bring spiritual advice and comfort whenever he can, the Cardinal has been busy perverting the course of justice by shielding his relative Grimaldi, even though he knows that the latter has murdered the entirely innocent Bergetto. Whichever woman the Cardinal means, therefore, we are not necessarily likely to agree with him.

However, that does not mean that the ambiguity is unimportant. Although on stage it could be resolved easily enough by having the Cardinal actually point at Putana, or gesture offstage towards where the corpse of Annabella may be presumed to be, perhaps it would be more useful to allow the audience to wonder for a moment who actually *is* 'chief in these effects'. In short, whose fault is it? The Cardinal has no trouble finding someone to blame and summing up events, glibly tossing off the concluding couplet, which gives the play its title: 'Of one so young, so rich in nature's store, / Who could not say, 'tis pity she's a whore?' Ford himself seems to have felt nervous about this phrase, since in his dedication of the play to the Earl of Peterborough he writes, 'The gravity of the subject may easily excuse the lightness of the title, otherwise I had been a severe judge against mine own guilt'. Actually one might have thought the opposite – that a grave subject would be better fitted by a grave title – but the fact that the phrase stands at the head of the play, appears as its last line, *and* is commented on by the author himself, suggests that it deserves attention.

The phrase insists that even if we condemn Annabella as a whore – which she is, in the Renaissance sense of someone who is neither a virgin nor a widow at the time of her marriage — we should recognise that it is a pity that she is so. So why has it happened? As with modern ideas about criminal behaviour, there are essentially two possible explanations for the disastrous careers of Giovanni and Annabella: either they are innately wicked, or their behaviour has been conditioned by society and thus society is, at least in part, responsible for their actions. The earliest critics of Ford thought that Giovanni and Annabella were indeed evil and abhorrent, and were worried that Ford himself did not seem necessarily to share their opinion. As in his later play *Perkin Warbeck*, where Ford refuses ever to make clear that Perkin Warbeck was an impostor and not the rightful king of England, so here he withholds any direct condemnation of Giovanni's and Annabella's love, and thus was repeatedly accused by early critics of glorifying incest. Though it is hard to see the last act, in particular, as any kind of celebration of incest, it is nevertheless true that it is equally hard to read or watch the play without feeling at least some degree of sympathy for Giovanni and Annabella, whatever one may feel about the advisability or morality of their behaviour.

Incest

One reason for this, of course, could be that their incest might not seem to belong to the realm of morality at all. Unlike the abuse of a child by a parent, brother-sister incest can be seen as consensual and victimless. It is taboo because inbreeding can produce deformed children, but intermarriage has also been the traditional tactic used by ruling families from the Egyptian Pharaohs to the Habsburgs to cement power within the dynasty. Giovanni himself alludes to this when he calls Annabella his Juno, reminding a mythologic-ally informed audience that incest is commonplace in stories

of the classical gods (as well as being a staple feature of all
creation myths and myths of origin, which typically postulate
one originating couple from whom all subsequent humans
are descended: whom did Adam and Eve's children marry?).
But gods and rulers are one thing, and ordinary people
another; perhaps Giovanni and Annabella's real crime, in
their society, is not so much to commit incest as to commit
incest while belonging, as Hippolita spitefully observes of
Annabella, merely to the merchant class.

This brings us back to the question of society, and of its
rôle in events. As well as the question-mark over whom the
Cardinal means by 'this woman', one other aspect of his
final dispensing of justice seems worthy of note. Whoever it
is that is to be burned is to 'be ta'en / Out of the city, for
example's sake'. And if he seems unnecessarily harsh in this
instance, he might well seem surprisingly lenient when he
dismisses Vasques with simply, 'Fellow, for thee, since what
thou didst was done / Not for thyself, being no Italian, /
We banish thee forever'. In the context of murder and incest,
two things against which there is a virtually universal pro-
hibition that some might see as rooted in 'human nature',
the stress on civic communities and specific nationalities
might seem surprising.

However, this emphasis is not new. In a small but significant
scene, III, ix, we have earlier seen the civic officers power-
less to pursue Grimaldi when he enters the grounds of the
Cardinal. This scene, set at the Cardinal's gate, shows us
individuals as being simply pawns in the tussle between civic
and religious authorities. Moreover, though the Cardinal
seems to think it a punishment to be expelled from the city,
we are made very aware of the stresses of city life, with
Annabella unable to find privacy and living under virtual
siege by her suitors. In Shakespeare's comedies (*As You Like*

It is a good example), there is a characteristic escape from
city life to a 'green world' where resolution can occur; in
'Tis Pity, there is no such possibility. This is one area in
which Giuseppe Patroni Griffi's 1973 film of the play, with
its isolated farmhouse and lush countryside, is seriously
misleading, since the play is actually so rooted in the
experiences of urban living that more than one critic has
termed it a 'city tragedy'. The same, of course, is true of
Romeo and Juliet, the play which *'Tis Pity She's a Whore*, with
its lovers, nurse and friar, virtually rewrites, as the Baz
Luhrmann film, *Romeo + Juliet*, with all its trappings of
high-pressure city life and fast communication, clearly
captures. And Annabella's and Giovanni's story does not
unfold in isolation any more than Romeo and Juliet's does;
we judge Annabella and Giovanni in the context within
which they live and against the poverty of example set to
them by those around them, so it is unsurprising if, although
they are so much more guilty than Romeo and Juliet, we
still sympathise with them.

Gender

Possibly, though, we may sympathise with Annabella rather
more than with Giovanni. The sensational nature of the
play's events may tend to draw our attention away from
Ford's approach to characterisation, but he certainly invites
us to see differences between the behaviour of Giovanni
and Annabella. Giovanni tells a direct lie when he informs
Annabella, 'I have asked counsel of the holy church, / Who
tells me I may love you' (I.ii.242-3), and at the close he
oscillates between bravado and near-madness when he first
arrogates to himself dominion over life and death and then
demands insanely whether anybody present recognises
Annabella's heart. Annabella, by contrast, is almost painfully

honest, carefully promising Soranzo nothing more than 'to live with you and yours'. She also seems to grow in moral stature throughout the play, and by the end to have acquired a distinctly spiritual perspective. When Giovanni visits her for the last time, she says to him, 'know that now there's but a dining-time / 'Twixt us and our confusion' (V.v.17-18). Uncorrected copies of the quarto, however, have the interesting variant 'dying-time', not 'dining-time', and although our edition follows the precedent of earlier editors, the earlier version may actually be more congruent with Annabella's growing interest in things spiritual: for her, what matters now is the life beyond, and dying could well be seen as only a prelude to that. It is certainly notable that although she is one of the relatively few women in Renaissance drama who actually does commit both incest and adultery rather than being merely suspected of one or both, she dies forgiven by the Friar and confident of heaven, whereas Giovanni, who seems to have learned nothing during the course of the play, has little more than a pagan afterlife in view.

One reason why Ford himself seems to treat Annabella more favourably than he does Giovanni may arise from his grasp of the fact that his own society would have made precisely the opposite decision, as is indeed suggested by the fact that both the Cardinal and the title of the play pass judgement on her but are silent on the subject of Giovanni. There certainly seems little reason for the inclusion of Philotis in the play except to reinforce the point that the constraints on women are far greater than those on men, though Philotis at least never does anything that might suggest that this discrepancy is justified; and it is similarly clear that while Hippolita suffers for her extramarital relationship with Soranzo, he himself continues to be regarded as a suitable match for a young and apparently innocent girl. Throughout the play, then, it is made clear that there is a double standard in operation in this society.

Bodies and Souls

The reason for this double standard is, of course, a collective social attempt to ensure that a woman's children really are fathered by her husband, and that men are not tricked into providing for and transmitting their property to the children of another man. Renaissance plays record a widespread paranoia about female fidelity and the legitimacy of offspring. It is sometimes suggested that this was an anxiety felt with particular urgency in the early part of the seventeenth century because of the growth of capitalism, though this seems too sweeping an explanation, and one not sufficiently confined to this period, to be very plausible. Another possible underlying cause lay in the inscrutability of the processes of conception and birth. It is difficult in our age of antenatal care and ultrasound to understand quite how little people once knew about how babies were made, and although this was an age with a fast-growing interest in medicine and anatomy, prompted partly by William Harvey's sensational discovery of the circulation of the blood, the dissection of a pregnant woman was, understandably, felt to be a desecration. Quite a bit is made in the play of the difficulties of understanding and policing this aspect of the female body: when Putana first tells him that Annabella is pregnant, Giovanni demands, 'With child? How dost thou know't?' (III.iv.10), and Vasques declares, ''Sfoot, if the lower parts of a she-tailor's cunning can cover such a swelling in the stomach, I'll never blame a false stitch in a shoe whiles I live again' (IV.iii.169-171). There is, moreover, a notable amount of talk in the play about matters of sickness and health: immediately before she herself is taken ill, Annabella affects to believe that Soranzo has been so, and Richardetto, for no reason of which we are ever informed, chooses the unusual and, one might have thought, risky disguise of pretending to be a doctor. This emphasis on the physical side of the human body reaches its climax when Giovanni, in his search for the truth of the metaphorical heart, literally looks inside an actual one.

It seems, then, that Ford is interested in the relationship between the physical and the psychological. This is certainly a recurrent topic of interest elsewhere in his plays. His tragicomedy *The Lover's Melancholy*, published in 1629, draws heavily on Robert Burton's vast book *The Anatomy of Melancholy* (1621), and offers a classification of the various types and causes of melancholy, together with an extended consideration of whether the roots of the condition lie in the body or the mind. Indeed all Ford's plays can be seen as exploring, to a lesser or greater extent, states of mind so unusual as to seem pathological: *The Broken Heart* centres on self-denial and self-punishment, *Perkin Warbeck* has as its hero a man who seems genuinely, though mistakenly, to believe that he is king of England, and in *The Fancies Chaste and Noble* two men, for different reasons, pretend to be impotent. In *'Tis Pity She's a Whore*, two people create for themselves a private world in which they apparently either forget or take no thought for the consequences which are likely to ensue from their transgression against the rules of society, and at least one of them seems to come very close to madness as a result.

Giovanni himself offers a strikingly physicalised account of his incestuous feelings in his opening conversation with the Friar. To Giovanni, the 'peevish sound' of mere words pales into insignificance beside the curiously concretised 'links of blood'. The word blood meant many things in the

seventeenth century in general and in *'Tis Pity She's a Whore*
in particular, since it occurs there more than thirty times. It
signifies, amongst other things, passion, family connections,
high birth, as well as the vital fluid without which life
would be impossible. This insistent repetition, along with
that of the word 'heart', which is heard even more
frequently before being so grotesquely literalised at the end,
raises the disturbing question of how much of our identity
as humans is constituted by our bodies rather than by our
minds or souls. Annabella believes in souls; Giovanni is
interested only in being able still to see her face, and by
the very nature of the thing, we cannot follow them beyond
death to know which is right.

Knowledge and Faith

Actually one of the most interesting points of the play is
its focus on what we can and cannot know. Even more
than about heart and blood, this play talks about knowing.
'Know' itself occurs seventy-six times, 'knowledge' three,
'know't' six, 'known' four, 'knows' three, 'knew' five, and
'know'st' four, giving a total of a hundred and two
instances. Ideas of knowledge, blindness, and ignorance
form an important part of the play's thematic structure.
There are, as in so many Renaissance plays, many puns
on the idea of 'carnal knowledge', and as well as Annabella
and Giovanni themselves, we also meet the people who
have been responsible for their respective educations, and
see them in the actual process of imparting instruction and
advice. What they claim to know, however, may well make
us feel that neither of them is a particularly suitable
instructor for the young. Putana talks about nothing but
sex, and the Friar, surprisingly, turns out to be more
interested in not knowing than in knowing, saying things

like 'No more; I may not hear it' (I.i.1-12), 'would mine ears / Had been one minute deaf, before the hour / That thou cam'st to me', (II.v.3-5) and 'I must not stay / To know thy fall… / would I had never known thee, / Or aught of thine' (V.iii.65-9). There is a striking contrast here with the Cardinal, who is happy to insist on the importance of what he knows, and for whom, indeed, the thing which is actually known seems to be less important than the fact that *he* knows it: he tells Donado not to pursue Bergetto's death further because 'we have knowledge on't. / Let that suffice' (III.ix.38-9). Similarly, Bergetto is happy to accept that the girl he has met must be Philotis because Florio says so. Ultimately, it is not what is known but who knows it that counts, and with these question-marks hanging over all the judgements offered us in the play, we must make up our own minds, about what, by the end of it, we think and know.

Staging the Play

It is perhaps because of this openness to interpretation that *'Tis Pity She's a Whore* has remained one of the more frequently staged of Renaissance plays. It was first acted at the Phoenix theatre (also known as the Cockpit) in Drury Lane by the Queen's Men. Like all acting companies at the time, the Queen's Men was entirely male, so the parts of Annabella, Philotis, Hippolyta and Putana will have been taken by boy actors (the company had four of these, so Ford has included as many female characters as his resources permitted.) It is difficult to gauge the effect of this, but the frontispiece of Beaumont and Fletcher's *Philaster*, in which the heroine Arethusa is depicted with one breast bare, suggests that audiences largely overlooked the fact of the boy actors' actual gender and imagined them as women. Moreover, the Phoenix was an indoor theatre, lit by candles, so visibility will not have been as good as at outdoor playhouses like the Globe. Admission prices were higher than at the Globe, though, resulting in a wealthy, sophisticated audience, many of whom were, like Ford himself, associated with the Inns of Court. The indoor playhouses also had more elaborate scenery and costumes, since these did not risk being spoiled by the rain. For the central stage prop of *'Tis Pity*, Annabella's heart, the obvious choice then, as now, was a sheep's heart – sufficiently bloody to supply a frisson, and also, for a Jacobean audience, unpleasantly recognisable as something they might eat.

More recent productions have, of course, used actresses rather than actors, and indeed the role of Annabella has proved very attractive, with Charlotte Rampling taking the role in Giuseppe Patroni Griffi's 1971 film version, which starred Oliver Tobias as Giovanni, and Cherie Lunghi playing her in a 1980 BBC TV version. In both of these the Bergetto sub-plot was entirely cut, and the Patroni Griffi film also shed much of Ford's language, focusing instead on imagery and on close-ups of its young, handsome lovers, innocents in a world of cynicism and sin. Amongst several recent stage productions, particularly notable were Yvonne Brewster's all-black cast at the Lyric Theatre, Hammersmith in 1995, and David Lan's at the Young Vic in 1999, with Jude Law as Giovanni and Eve Best in her professional debut as Annabella in a production in which it was, once more, quite clear that the brother and sister were not evil but were the victims of a corrupt society.

For Further Reading

The only recent monograph on Ford is Lisa Hopkins, *John Ford's Political Theatre* (1994), which argues that Ford's plays encode resentment against the government of Charles I and sympathy for Catholicism. Two edited collections marked the quatercentenary of his birth in 1586, Donald K. Anderson jr's *'Concord in Discord': The Plays of John Ford, 1586-1986* (1986), and Michael Neill's *John Ford: Critical Re-Visions* (1988); both contain a variety of strong essays. Marion Lomax's *Stage Images and Traditions: Shakespeare to Ford* (1987) situates Ford's emblematic drama within the context of his time, and Rowland Wymer's *Webster and Ford* (1995) offers a sensitive analysis of the effect of his plays.

Ford: Key Dates

1586 Born to Thomas Ford and Elizabeth Popham in Ilsington, Devon.

1602 Admitted to the Middle Temple. Not known ever to have left it thereafter except for a period of expulsion from 1606-8 for failing to pay his buttery bill. May have travelled at some stage but nothing firm is known.

1606 Published *Fame's Memorial*, an elegy on the Earl of Devonshire, and *Honour Triumphant*, a prose piece.

1613 *Christ's Bloody Sweat* (poem) and *The Golden Mean* (prose tract) published.

1620 *A Line of Life* (prose tract).

1621 Publication of *The Witch of Edmonton*, co-written by Ford, Thomas Dekker, and William Rowley. Around the same period he seems also to have collaborated with Dekker on *The Sun's Darling*, *The Welsh Ambassador*, and *The Spanish Gipsy*, and possibly on other plays, though these were not published until the 1650s.

1629 *The Lover's Melancholy* published.

1633 *'Tis Pity She's a Whore*, *The Broken Heart* and *Love's Sacrifice* published.

1634 *Perkin Warbeck* published.

1638 *The Fancies Chaste and Noble* published. *The Lady's Trial* produced.

1639 *The Lady's Trial* published. Nothing further is heard of Ford and he is assumed to have died shortly after.

1653 Publication of *The Queen*, an anonymous play probably by Ford.

'TIS PITY SHE'S A WHORE

[Dramatis Personae]

GIOVANNI, *a young gentleman of Parma*
ANNABELLA, *his sister*
FRIAR BONAVENTURA, *formerly tutor to Giovanni*
PUTANA, *Annabella's governess*
THE CARDINAL
RICHARDETTO, *supposed to be dead but actually disguised as a doctor*
PHILOTIS, *his niece*
HIPPOLITA, *his unfaithful wife*
GRIMALDI, *a Roman gentleman, follower of the Cardinal and suitor of Annabella*
SORANZO, *a nobleman, suitor of Annabella and former lover of Hippolyta*
VASQUES, *his servant*
BERGETTO, *a foolish young man and suitor of Annabella*
POGGIO, *his servant*
FLORIO, *a citizen of Parma, father of Giovanni and Annabella*
DONADO, *another citizen, uncle of Bergetto*
BANDITTI

The setting is Parma.

[I.i]

Enter GIOVANNI *and* FRIAR BONAVENTURA

FRIAR.
> Dispute no more in this, for know, young man,
> These are no school points. Nice philosophy
> May tolerate unlikely arguments,
> But Heaven-admits no jest; wits that presumed
> On wit too much, by striving how to prove
> There was no God, with foolish grounds of art,
> Discovered first the nearest way to Hell
> And filled the world with devilish atheism.
> Such questions, youth, are fond; for better 'tis
> To bless the sun than reason why it shines;
> Yet he thou talk'st of is above the sun.
> No more; I may not hear it.

GIOVANNI.   Gentle father,
> To you I have unclasped my burdened soul,
> Emptied the store-house of my thoughts and heart,
> Made myself poor of secrets; have not left
> Another word untold, which hath not spoke
> All what I ever durst, or think, or know;
> And yet is here the comfort I shall have,
> Must I not do what all men else may, love?

FRIAR. Yes, you may love, fair son.

GIOVANNI.   Must I not praise
> That beauty which, if framed anew, the gods

Would make a god of, if they had it there,
And kneel to it, as I do kneel to them?

FRIAR. Why, foolish madman!

GIOVANNI.   Shall a peevish sound,
   A customary form from man to man
   Of brother and of sister, be a bar
   Twixt my perpetual happiness and me?
   Say that we had one father, say one womb –
   Curse to my joys! – gave both us life, and birth;
   Are we not therefore each to other bound
   So much the more by nature, by the links
   Of blood, of reason – nay, if you will have it,
   Even of religion – to be ever one,
   One soul, one flesh, one love, one heart, one all?

FRIAR. Have done, unhappy youth, for thou art lost.

GIOVANNI. Shall then, for that I am her brother born,
   My joys be ever banished from her bed?
   No, father; in your eyes I see the change
   Of pity and compassion; from your age,
   As from a sacred oracle, distills
   The life of counsel; tell me, holy man,
   What cure shall give me ease in these extremes?

FRIAR. Repentance, son, and sorrow for this sin;
   For thou hast moved a Majesty above
   With thy unrangèd (almost) blasphemy.

GIOVANNI. Oh, do not speak of that, dear confessor.

FRIAR. Art thou, my son, that miracle of wit,
   Who once within these three months wert esteemed
   A wonder of thine age throughout Bononia?
   How did the university applaud
   Thy government, behaviour, learning, speech,

Sweetness, and all that could make up a man!
I was proud of my tutelage, and chose
Rather to leave my books than part with thee.
I did so; but the fruits of all my hopes
Are lost in thee, as thou art in thyself.
Oh, Giovanni, hast thou left the schools
Of knowledge, to converse with lust and death?
For death waits on thy lust. Look through the world,
And thou shalt see a thousand faces shine
More glorious than this idol thou ador'st.
Leave her, and take thy choice; 'tis much less sin,
Though in such games as those, they lose that win.

GIOVANNI. It were more easy to stop the ocean
From floats and ebbs, than to dissuade my vow.

FRIAR. Then I have done, and in thy wilful flames
Already see thy ruin; Heaven is just.
Yet hear my counsel.

GIOVANNI.   As a voice of life.

FRIAR. Hie to thy father's house; there lock thee fast
Alone within thy chamber, then fall down
On both thy knees, and grovel on the ground;
Cry to thy heart, wash every word thou utter'st
In tears, and (if't be possible) of blood;
Beg Heaven to cleanse the leprosy of lust
That rots thy soul; acknowledge what thou art,
A wretch, a worm, a nothing; weep, sigh, pray
Three times a day, and three times every night.
For seven days' space do this. Then, if thou find'st
No change in thy desires, return to me:
I'll think on remedy. Pray for thyself
At home, whilst I pray for thee here. Away,
My blessing with thee, we have need to pray.

GIOVANNI. All this I'll do, to free me from the rod
  Of vengeance; else I'll swear my Fate's my God.

  Exeunt.

[I.ii]

Enter GRIMALDI *and* VASQUES *ready to fight.*

VASQUES. Come sir, stand to your tackling; if you prove
  craven, I'll make you run quickly.

GRIMALDI. Thou art no equal match for me.

VASQUES. Indeed I never went to the wars to bring home
  news, nor cannot play the mountebank for a meal's meat,
  and swear I got my wounds in the field. See you these
  grey hairs? They'll not flinch for a bloody nose; wilt thou
  to this gear?

GRIMALDI. Why, slave, think'st thou I'll balance my
  reputation with a cast-suit? Call thy master, he shall know
  that I dare –

VASQUES. Scold like a cot-quean; that's your profession,
  thou poor shadow of a soldier. I will make thee know, my
  master keeps servants thy betters in quality and
  performance. Com'st thou to fight or prate?

GRIMALDI. Neither with thee. I am a Roman and a
  gentleman, one that have got mine honour with expense
  of blood.

VASQUES. You are a lying coward, and a fool. Fight, or,
  by these hilts, I'll kill thee. Brave my lord, you'll fight.

GRIMALDI. Provoke me not, for if thou dost −

They fight. GRIMALDI *hath the worst.*

VASQUES. Have at you.

Enter FLORIO, DONADO, *and* SORANZO.

FLORIO. What mean these sudden broils so near my doors?
    Have you not other places but my house
    To vent the spleen of your disordered bloods?
    Must I be haunted still with such unrest
    As not to eat or sleep in peace at home?
    Is this your love, Grimaldi? Fie, 'tis naught.

DONADO. And Vasques, I may tell thee 'tis not well
    To broach these quarrels; you are ever forward
    In seconding contentions.

Enter above ANNABELLA *and* PUTANA.

FLORIO.   What's the ground?

SORANZO. That, with your patience, Signors, I'll resolve:
    This gentleman, whom fame reports a soldier
    (For else I know not), rivals me in love
    To Signor Florio's daughter; to whose ears
    He still prefers his suit, to my disgrace,
    Thinking the way to recommend himself
    Is to disparage me in his report:
    But know, Grimaldi, though (maybe) thou art
    My equal in thy blood, yet this bewrays
    A lowness in thy mind which, wert thou noble,
    Thou would'st as much disdain as I do thee
    For this unworthiness; and on this ground
    I will'd my servant to correct his tongue,
    Holding a man so base no match for me.

VASQUES. And had your sudden coming not prevented us,

I had let my gentleman blood under the gills; I should
have worm'd you, sir, for running mad.

GRIMALDI. I'll be revenged, Soranzo.

VASQUES. On a dish of warm broth to stay your stomach,
do, honest innocence, do; spoon-meat is a wholesomer
diet than a Spanish blade.

GRIMALDI. Remember this.

SORANZO. I fear thee not, Grimaldi.

Exit GRIMALDI.

FLORIO. My Lord Soranzo, this is strange to me,
Why you should storm, having my word engaged:
Owing her heart, what need you doubt her ear?
Losers may talk, by law, of any game.

VASQUES. Yet the villainy of words, Signior Florio, may be
such as would make any unspleened dove choleric. Blame
not my lord in this.

FLORIO. Be you more silent.
I would not for my wealth my daughter's love
Should cause the spilling of one drop of blood.
Vasques, put up, let's end this fray in wine.

Exeunt.

PUTANA. How like you this, child? Here's threatening,
challenging, quarrelling and fighting on every side, and
all is for your sake; you had need look to yourself,
charge, you'll be stolen away sleeping else shortly.

ANNABELLA. But, tut'ress, such a life gives no content
To me; my thoughts are fixed on other ends.
Would you would leave me.

PUTANA. Leave you? No marvel else; leave me no leaving, charge,

this is love outright. Indeed I blame you not, you have choice fit for the best lady in Italy.

ANNABELLA. Pray do not talk so much.

PUTANA. Take the worst with the best, there's Grimaldi the soldier, a very well-timbered fellow. They say he is a Roman, nephew to the Duke Mount Ferratto. They say he did good service in the wars against the Milanese; but faith, charge, I do not like him, and it be for nothing, but for being a soldier; there's not one amongst twenty of your skirmishing captains, but have some privy maim or other that mars their standing upright. I like him the worse, he crinkles so much in the hams; though he might serve, if there were no more men, yet he's not the man I would choose.

ANNABELLA. Fie, how thou prat'st.

PUTANA. As I am a very woman, I like Signior Soranzo well; he is wise, and what is more, rich; and what is more than that, kind, and what is more than all this, a nobleman. Such a one, were I the fair Annabella my self, I would wish and pray for. Then he is bountiful; besides he is handsome, and, by my troth, I think wholesome (and that's news in a gallant of three and twenty); liberal, that I know; loving, that you know; and a man, sure, else he could never have purchased such a good name with Hippolita the lusty widow in her husband's lifetime. And t'were but for that report, sweetheart, would 'a were thine: commend a man for his qualities, but take a husband as he is a plain-sufficient, naked man; such a one is for your bed, and such a one is Signior Soranzo, my life for't.

ANNABELLA. Sure the woman took her morning's draught too soon.

Enter BERGETTO *and* POGGIO.

PUTANA. But look, sweetheart, look what thing comes now: here's another of your ciphers to fill up the number. Oh brave old ape in a silken coat! Observe.

BERGETTO. Didst thou think, Poggio, that I would spoil my new clothes, and leave my dinner, to fight?

POGGIO. No, sir, I did not take you for so arrant a baby.

BERGETTO. I am wiser than so; for I hope, Poggio, thou never heardst of an elder brother that was a coxcomb, didst Poggio?

POGGIO. Never indeed, sir, as long as they had either land or money left them to inherit.

BERGETTO. Is it possible, Poggio? Oh, monstrous! Why, I'll undertake with a handful of silver to buy a headful of wit at any time; but sirrah, I have another purchase in hand: I shall have the wench, mine uncle says. I will but wash my face, and shift socks, and then have at her i'faith – Mark my pace, Poggio.

POGGIO. Sir, I have seen an ass and a mule trot the Spanish pavan with a better grace, I know not how often.

Exeunt.

ANNABELLA. This idiot haunts me too.

PUTANA. Ay, ay, he needs no description. The rich magnifico that is below with your father, charge, Signior Donado his uncle, for that he means to make this his cousin a golden calf, thinks that you will be a right Israelite, and fall down to him presently; but I hope I have

tutored you better. They say a fool's bauble is a lady's
playfellow: yet you having wealth enough, you need not
cast upon the dearth of flesh, at any rate. Hang him,
innocent.

Enter GIOVANNI.

ANNABELLA. But see, Putana, see: what blessed shape
Of some celestial creature now appears?
What man is he, that with such sad aspect
Walks careless of himself?

PUTANA.   Where?

ANNABELLA.   Look below.

PUTANA. Oh, 'tis your brother, sweet –

ANNABELLA.   Ha!

PUTANA.   'Tis your brother.

ANNABELLA. Sure 'tis not he; this is some woeful thing
Wrapped up in grief, some shadow of a man.
Alas, he beats his breast, and wipes his eyes,
Drowned all in tears; methinks I hear him sigh.
Let's down, Putana, and partake the cause;
I know my brother, in the love he bears me,
Will not deny me partage in his sadness.
My soul is full of heaviness and fear.

Exeunt.

GIOVANNI. Lost, I am lost; my fates have doomed my
death.
The more I strive, I love; the more I love,
The less I hope; I see my ruin certain.
What judgement or endeavours could apply
To my incurable and restless wounds

I throughly have examined, but in vain.
O that it were not in religion sin
To make our love a God, and worship it!
I have even wearied heaven with prayers, dried up
The spring of my continual tears, even starved
My veins with daily fasts; what wit or art
Could counsel, I have practised; but, alas,
I find all these but dreams, and old men's tales
To fright unsteady youth. I'm still the same.
Or I must speak, or burst; 'tis not, I know,
My lust, but 'tis my fate that leads me on.
Keep fear and low faint-hearted shame with slaves,
I'll tell her that I love her, though my heart
Were rated at the price of that attempt.
Oh me! she comes.

Enter ANNABELLA *and* PUTANA.

ANNABELLA.   Brother.

GIOVANNI.   If such a thing
    As courage dwell in men, ye heavenly powers,
    Now double all that virtue in my tongue.

ANNABELLA. Why, brother, will you not speak to me?

GIOVANNI.   Yes.
    How d'ee, sister?

ANNABELLA. Howsoever I am, methinks you are not well.

PUTANA. Bless us, why are you so sad, sir?

GIOVANNI. Let me entreat you leave us a while, Putana.
    Sister, I would be private with you.

ANNABELLA. Withdraw, Putana.

PUTANA. I will. [*Aside.*] If this were any other company for her, I should think my absence an office of some credit, but I will leave them together.

Exit PUTANA.

GIOVANNI. Come, sister, lend your hand; let's walk together.
I hope you need not blush to walk with me;
Here's none but you and I.

ANNABELLA. How's this?

GIOVANNI. Faith, I mean no harm.

ANNABELLA. Harm?

GIOVANNI. No, good faith; how is't with'ee?

ANNABELLA. [*Aside.*] I trust he be not frantic – I am very well, brother.

GIOVANNI. Trust me, but I am sick; I fear so sick
'Twill cost my life.

ANNABELLA. Mercy forbid it! 'Tis not so, I hope.

GIOVANNI. I think you love me, sister.

ANNABELLA. Yes, you know I do.

GIOVANNI. I know't indeed – y'are very fair.

ANNABELLA. Nay then, I see you have a merry sickness.

GIOVANNI. That's as it proves. The poets feign, I read,
That Juno for her forehead did exceed
All other goddesses; but I durst swear
Your forehead exceeds hers, as hers did theirs.

ANNABELLA. Troth, this is pretty.

GIOVANNI.   Such a pair of stars

As are thine eyes would, like Promethean fire,
If gently glanced, give life to senseless stones.

ANNABELLA. Fie upon 'ee.

GIOVANNI. The lily and the rose, most sweetly strange,
Upon your dimpled cheeks do strive for change.
Such lips would tempt a saint; such hands as those
Would make an anchorite lascivious.

ANNABELLA. D'ee mock me, or flatter me?

GIOVANNI. If you would see a beauty more exact
Than art can counterfeit or nature frame,
Look in your glass, and there behold your own.

ANNABELLA. Oh, you are a trim youth.

GIOVANNI. Here.

Offers his dagger to her.

ANNABELLA.   What to do?

GIOVANNI.   And here's my breast, strike home.
Rip up my bosom; there thou shalt behold
A heart in which is writ the truth I speak.
Why stand 'ee?

ANNABELLA.   Are you earnest?

GIOVANNI.   Yes, most earnest.
You cannot love?

ANNABELLA.   Whom?

GIOVANNI.   Me. My tortured soul
Hath felt affliction in the heat of Death.
O Annabella, I am quite undone.
The love of thee, my sister, and the view

Of thy immortal beauty hath untuned
All harmony both of my rest and life.
Why d'ee not strike?

ANNABELLA.   Forbid it my just fears.
If this be true, 'twere fitter I were dead.

GIOVANNI. True, Annabella; 'tis no time to jest.
I have too long suppressed the hidden flames
That almost have consumed me; I have spent
Many a silent night in sighs and groans,
Run over all my thoughts, despised my fate,
Reasoned against the reasons of my love,
Done all that smooth-cheeked virtue could advise,
But found all bootless; 'tis my destiny
That you must either love, or I must die.

ANNABELLA. Comes this in sadness from you?

GIOVANNI.   Let some mischief
Befall me soon, if I dissemble ought.

ANNABELLA. You are my brother, Giovanni.

GIOVANNI.   You,
My sister, Annabella; I know this,
And could afford you instance why to love
So much the more for this; to which intent
Wise Nature first in your creation meant
To make you mine; else 't had been sin and foul,
To share one beauty to a double soul.
Nearness in birth or blood doth but persuade
A nearer nearness in affection.
I have asked counsel of the holy Church,
Who tells me I may love you; and 'tis just,
That since I may, I should; and will, yea, will;
Must I now live, or die?

ANNABELLA.   Live. Thou hast won
  The field, and never fought; what thou hast urged,
  My captive heart had long ago resolved.
  I blush to tell thee, but I'll tell thee now,
  For every sigh that thou hast spent for me,
  I have sighed ten; for every tear shed twenty;
  And not so much for that I loved, as that
  I durst not say I loved, nor scarcely think it.

GIOVANNI. Let not this music be a dream, ye gods,
  For pity's sake I beg 'ee.

ANNABELLA.   On my knees,
  [*She kneels.*]
  Brother, even by our mother's dust, I charge you,
  Do not betray me to your mirth or hate,
  Love me, or kill me, brother.

GIOVANNI.   On my knees,

  [*He kneels.*]

  Sister, even by my mother's dust I charge you,
  Do not betray me to your mirth or hate,
  Love me, or kill me, sister.

ANNABELLA. You mean good sooth then?

GIOVANNI.   In good troth I do,
  And so do you, I hope; say 'I'm in earnest'.

ANNABELLA. I'll swear't, I.

GIOVANNI.   And I, and by this kiss,

  [*Kisses her.*]

  Once more, yet once more – now let's rise – by this,
  I would not change this minute for Elysium.
  What must we now do?

ANNABELLA.   What you will.

GIOVANNI.   Come then.
   After so many tears as we have wept,
   Let's learn to court in smiles, to kiss, and sleep.

Exeunt.

[I.iii]

Enter FLORIO *and* DONADO.

FLORIO. Signior Donado, you have said enough.
   I understand you, but would have you know
   I will not force my daughter 'gainst her will.
   You see I have but two, a son and her;
   And he is so devoted to his book
   As, I must tell you true, I doubt his health;
   Should he miscarry, all my hopes rely
   Upon my girl. As for worldly fortune,
   I am, I thank my stars, blessed with enough;
   My care is how to match her to her liking.
   I would not have her marry wealth, but love,
   And if she like your nephew, let him have her;
   Here's all that I can say.

DONADO.   Sir, you say well,
   Like a true father, and for my part, I,
   If the young folks can like ('twixt you and me),
   Will promise to assure my nephew presently
   Three thousand florins yearly during life,
   And after I am dead, my whole estate.

FLORIO. 'Tis a fair proffer, sir. Meantime, your nephew
   Shall have free passage to commence his suit;

If he can thrive, he shall have my consent.
So for this time I'll leave you, Signior.

Exit FLORIO.

DONADO.   Well,
Here's hope yet, if my nephew would have wit;
But he is such another dunce, I fear
He'll never win the wench. When I was young
I could have done't, i'faith, and so shall he
If he will learn of me; and in good time
He comes himself.

Enter BERGETTO *and* POGGIO.

How now, Bergetto, whither away so fast?

BERGETTO. Oh, uncle, I have heard the strangest news
that ever came out of the mint, have I not, Poggio?

POGGIO. Yes indeed, sir.

DONADO. What news, Bergetto?

BERGETTO. Why, look ye, uncle, my barber told me just
now that there is a fellow come to town, who undertakes
to make a mill go without the mortal help of any water
or wind, only with sand-bags; and this fellow hath a
strange horse, a most excellent beast, I'll assure you,
uncle (my barber says), whose head, to the wonder of all
Christian people, stands just behind where his tail is. Is't
not true, Poggio?

POGGIO. So the barber swore, forsooth.

DONADO. And you are running thither?

BERGETTO. Ay, forsooth, uncle.

DONADO. Wilt thou be a fool still? Come, sir, you shall
not go; you have more mind of a puppet-play than on

the business I told ye; why, thou great baby, wilt never
have wit, wilt make thyself a May-game to all the world?

POGGIO. Answer for yourself, master.

BERGETTO. Why, uncle, should I sit at home still, and
not go abroad to see fashions like other gallants?

DONADO. To see hobby-horses! What wise talk, I pray,
had you with Annabella, when you were at Signior
Florio's house?

BERGETTO. Oh, the wench: uds save me, uncle, I tickled
her with a rare speech, that I made her almost burst her
belly with laughing.

DONADO. Nay, I think so, and what speech was't?

BERGETTO. What did I say, Poggio?

POGGIO. Forsooth, my master said that he loved her
almost as well as he loved parmesan, and swore (I'll be
sworn for him) that she wanted but such a nose as his
was to be as pretty a young woman as any was in Parma.

DONADO. Oh gross!

BERGETTO. Nay, uncle, then she asked me whether my
father had any more children than my self: and I said no,
'twere better he should have had his brains knocked out
first.

DONADO. This is intolerable.

BERGETTO. Then said she, 'Will Signior Donado your
uncle leave you all his wealth?'

DONADO. Ha! That was good, did she harp upon that
string?

BERGETTO. Did she harp upon that string? Ay, that she
did: I answered, 'Leave me all his wealth? Why, woman,
he hath no other wit; if he had, he should hear on't to
his everlasting glory and confusion: I know,' (quoth I)
'I am his white boy, and will not be gulled'; and with
that she fell into a great smile, and went away. Nay, I did
fit her.

DONADO. Ah, sirrah, then I see there is no changing
of nature. Well, Bergetto, I fear thou wilt be a very
ass still.

BERGETTO. I should be sorry for that, uncle.

DONADO. Come, come you home with me; since you are
no better a speaker, I'll have you write to her after some
courtly manner, and enclose some rich jewel in the letter.

BERGETTO. Ay, marry, that will be excellent.

DONADO. Peace, innocent.
Once in my time I'll set my wits to school;
If all fail, 'tis but the fortune of a fool.

BERGETTO. Poggio, 'twill do, Poggio.

Exeunt.

[II.i]

Enter GIOVANNI *and* ANNABELLA, *as from their chamber.*

GIOVANNI. Come, Annabella; no more sister now,
  But love, a name more gracious; do not blush,
  Beauty's sweet wonder, but be proud to know
  That, yielding, thou hast conquered, and inflamed
  A heart whose tribute is thy brother's life.

ANNABELLA.
  And mine is his. Oh, how these stolen contents
  Would print a modest crimson on my cheeks,
  Had any but my heart's delight prevailed.

GIOVANNI. I marvel why the chaster of your sex
  Should think this pretty toy called maidenhead
  So strange a loss, when, being lost, 'tis nothing,
  And you are still the same.

ANNABELLA.   'Tis well for you,
  Now you can talk.

GIOVANNI. Music as well consists
  In th'ear, as in the playing.

ANNABELLA. Oh, y'are wanton;
  Tell on't, y'are best, do.

GIOVANNI.   Thou wilt chide me then.
  Kiss me, so; thus hung Jove on Leda's neck,
  And sucked divine ambrosia from her lips.
  I envy not the mightiest man alive,
  But hold myself, in being king of thee,

More great than were I king of all the world:
But I shall lose you, sweetheart.

ANNABELLA.   But you shall not.

GIOVANNI. You must be married, mistress.

ANNABELLA.   Yes, to whom?

GIOVANNI. Some one must have you.

ANNABELLA.   You must.

GIOVANNI.   Nay, some other.

ANNABELLA. Now prithee do not speak so without jesting;
You'll make me weep in earnest.

GIOVANNI.   What, you will not?
But tell me, sweet, canst thou be dared to swear
That thou wilt live to me, and to no other?

ANNABELLA. By both our loves I dare, for didst thou
know,
My Giovanni, how all suitors seem
To my eyes hateful, thou wouldst trust me then.

GIOVANNI. Enough, I take thy word. Sweet, we must part;
Remember what thou vow'st, keep well my heart.

ANNABELLA. Will you be gone?

GIOVANNI.   I must.

ANNABELLA.   When to return?

GIOVANNI. Soon.

ANNABELLA.   Look you do.

GIOVANNI.   Farewell.

Exit GIOVANNI.

ANNABELLA.
Go where thou wilt, in mind I'll keep thee here,
And where thou art, I know I shall be there.
Guardian!

Enter PUTANA.

PUTANA. Child, how is't, child? Well, thank Heaven, ha!

ANNABELLA. O guardian, what a paradise of joy
Have I passed over!

PUTANA. Nay, what a paradise of joy have you passed
under! Why, now I commend thee, charge; fear nothing,
sweetheart. What though he be your brother? your
brother's a man, I hope, and I say still, if a young wench
feel the fit upon her, let her take anybody, father or
brother, all is one.

ANNABELLA. I would not have it known for all the world.

PUTANA. Nor I, indeed, for the speech of the people; else
'twere nothing.

FLORIO [*within*]. Daughter Annabella!

ANNABELLA. O me! my father, – here, sir, – reach my
work.

FLORIO [*within*]. What are you doing?

ANNABELLA. So, let him come now.

Enter FLORIO, RICHARDETTO *disguised as a doctor, and*
PHILOTIS *with a lute in her hand.*

FLORIO. So hard at work, that's well; you lose no time.
Look, I have brought you company: here's one, a learned
doctor, lately come from Padua, much skilled in physic,
and for that I see you have of late been sickly, I entreated
this reverent man to visit you some time.

ANNABELLA. Y'are very welcome, sir.

RICHARDETTO.   I thank you, mistress.
  Loud fame in large report hath spoke your praise,
  As well for virtue as perfection:
  For which I have been bold to bring with me
  A kinswoman of mine, a maid, for song
  And music, one perhaps will give content;
  Please you to know her.

ANNABELLA.   They are parts I love,
  And she for them most welcome.

PHILOTIS.   Thank you, lady.

FLORIO.
  Sir, now you know my house, pray make not strange,
  And if you find my daughter need your art,
  I'll be your paymaster.

RICHARDETTO.   Sir, what I am
  She shall command.

FLORIO.   You shall bind me to you.
  Daughter, I must have conference with you,
  About some matters that concerns us both.
  Good master doctor, please you but walk in,
  We'll crave a little of your cousin's cunning.
  I think my girl hath not quite forgot
  To touch an instrument; she could have done't.
  We'll hear them both.

RICHARDETTO.   I'll wait upon you, sir.

  Exeunt.

[II.ii]

Enter SORANZO *in his study reading a book.*

SORANZO. 'Love's measure is extreme, the comfort, pain;
The life unrest, and the reward disdain.'
What's here? look o'er again; 'tis so, so writes
This smooth licentious poet in his rhymes.
But, Sanazar, thou liest, for had thy bosom
Felt such oppression as is laid on mine,
Thou wouldst have kissed the rod that made thee smart.
To work, then happy Muse, and contradict
What Sanazar hath in his envy writ.
'Love's measure is the mean, sweet his annoys,
His pleasures life, and his reward all joys.'
Had Annabella lived when Sanazar
Did in his brief enconium celebrate
Venice, that queen of cities, he had left
That verse which gained him such a sum of gold,
And for one only look from Annabell
Had writ of her, and her diviner cheeks.
O how my thoughts are –

VASQUES [*within*] Pray forbear; in rules of civility, let me
give notice on't: I shall be taxed of my neglect of duty
and service.

SORANZO. What rude intrusion interrupts my peace?
Can I be nowhere private?

VASQUES [*within*]. Troth, you wrong your modesty.

SORANZO. What's the matter, Vasques, who is't?

Enter HIPPOLITA *and* VASQUES.

HIPPOLITA.   'Tis I:

Do you know me now? Look, perjured man, on her
Whom thou and thy distracted lust have wrong'd.
Thy sensual rage of blood hath made my youth
A scorn to men and angels, and shall I
Be now a foil to thy unsated change?
Thou knowst, false wanton, when my modest fame
Stood free from stain or scandal, all the charms
Of Hell or sorcery could not prevail
Against the honour of my chaster bosom.
Thine eyes did plead in tears, thy tongue in oaths
Such and so many, that a heart of steel
Would have been wrought to pity, as was mine;
And shall the conquest of my lawful bed,
My husband's death urged on by his disgrace,
My loss of womanhood, be ill rewarded
With hatred and contempt? No, know, Soranzo,
I have a spirit doth as much distaste
The slavery of fearing thee, as thou
Dost loathe the memory of what hath passed.

SORANZO. Nay, dear Hippolita –

HIPPOLITA.   Call me not dear,
Nor think with supple words to smooth the grossness
Of my abuses; 'tis not your new mistress,
Your goodly Madam Merchant, shall triumph
On my dejection; tell her thus from me,
My birth was nobler, and by much more free.

SORANZO. You are too violent.

HIPPOLITA.   You are too double
In your dissimulation. See'st thou this,
This habit, these black mourning weeds of care?
'Tis thou art cause of this, and hast divorced
My husband from his life and me from him,
And made me widow in my widowhood.

SORANZO. Will you yet hear?

HIPPOLITA. More of thy perjuries?
Thy soul is drowned too deeply in those sins;
Thou need'st not add to the number.

SORANZO. Then I'll leave you,
You are past all rules of sense.

HIPPOLITA. And thou of grace.

VASQUES. Fie, mistress, you are not near the limits of
reason; if my lord had a resolution as noble as virtue
itself, you take the course to unedge it all. Sir, I beseech
you do not perplex her; griefs, alas, will have a vent.
I dare undertake Madam Hippolita will now freely hear
you.

SORANZO. Talk to a woman frantic? Are these the fruits
of your love?

HIPPOLITA. They are the fruits of thy untruth, false man.
Didst thou not swear, whilst yet my husband lived,
That thou wouldst wish no happiness on earth
More than to call me wife? Didst thou not vow,
When he should die, to marry me? For which
The devil in my blood, and thy protests,
Caused me to counsel him to undertake
A voyage to Ligorne, for that we heard
His brother there was dead, and left a daughter
Young and unfriended, who with much ado
I wished him to bring hither; he did so,
And went; and, as thou know'st, died on the way.
Unhappy man, to buy his death so dear
With my advice! Yet thou, for whom I did it,
Forget'st thy vows, and leav'st me to my shame.

SORANZO. Who could help this?

HIPPOLITA.   Who? Perjured man, thou couldst,
    If thou hadst faith or love.

SORANZO.   You are deceived.
    The vows I made, if you remember well,
    Were wicked and unlawful; 'twere more sin
    To keep them than to break them. As for me,
    I cannot mask my penitence. Think thou
    How much thou hast digressed from honest shame
    In bringing of a gentleman to death
    Who was thy husband; such a one as he,
    So noble in his quality, condition,
    Learning, behaviour, entertainment, love,
    As Parma could not show a braver man.

VASQUES. You do not well, this was not your promise.

SORANZO. I care not; let her know her monstrous life.
    Ere I'll be servile to so black a sin
    I'll be accursed; woman, come here no more.
    Learn to repent and die, for, by my honour,
    I hate thee and thy lust; you have been too foul.

    Exit SORANZO.

VASQUES. This part has been scurvily played.

HIPPOLITA. How foolishly this beast contemns his fate,
    And shuns the use of that which I more scorn
    Than I once loved, his love; but let him go.
    My vengeance shall give comfort to this woe.

    She starts to go away.

VASQUES. Mistress, mistress Madam Hippolita, pray a
    word or two.

HIPPOLITA.With me, sir?

VASQUES. With you, if you please.

HIPPOLITA. What is't?

VASQUES. I know you are infinitely moved now, and you think you have cause; some I confess you have, but sure not so much as you imagine.

HIPPOLITA. Indeed.

VASQUES. O you were miserably bitter, which you followed even to the last syllable; faith, you were somewhat too shrewd. By my life, you could not have took my lord in a worse time since I first knew him; tomorrow you shall find him a new man.

HIPPOLITA. Well, I shall wait his leisure.

VASQUES. Fie, this is not a hearty patience, it comes sourly from you. Troth, let me persuade you for once.

HIPPOLITA [*aside*]. I have it, and it shall be so; thanks, opportunity. [*To* VASQUES.] Persuade me to what?

VASQUES. Visit him in some milder temper. Oh, if you could but master a little your female spleen, how might you win him!

HIPPOLITA. He will never love me. Vasques, thou hast been a too trusty servant to such a master, and I believe thy reward in the end will fall out like mine.

VASQUES. So perhaps too.

HIPPOLITA. Resolve thyself it will; had I one so true, so truly honest, so secret to my counsels, as thou hast been to him and his, I should think it a slight acquittance, not only to make him master of all I have, but even of myself.

VASQUES. Oh, you are a noble gentlewoman.

HIPPOLITA. Wilt thou feed always upon hopes? Well, I know thou art wise, and seest the reward of an old servant daily, what it is.

VASQUES. Beggary and neglect.

HIPPOLITA. True, but Vasques, wert thou mine, and wouldst be private to me and my designs, I here protest myself, and all what I can else call mine, should be at thy dispose.

VASQUES [*Aside*]. Work you that way, old mole? Then I have the wind of you. [*To* HIPPOLITA.] I were not worthy of it, by any desert that could lie within my compass; if I could –

HIPPOLITA. What then?

VASQUES. I should then hope to live in these my old years with rest and security.

HIPPOLITA.
Give me thy hand; now promise but thy silence,
And help to bring to pass a plot I have;
And here in sight of Heaven, that being done,
I make thee lord of me and mine estate.

VASQUES. Come, you are merry; this is such a happiness that I can neither think or believe.

HIPPOLITA. Promise thy secrecy, and 'tis confirmed.

VASQUES. Then here I call our good genii for witnesses, whatsoever your designs are, or against whomsoever, I will not only be a special actor therein, but never disclose it till it be effected.

HIPPOLITA. I take thy word, and with that, thee for mine. Come then, let's more confer of this anon.

On this delicious bane my thoughts shall banquet:
Revenge shall sweeten what my griefs have tasted.

Exeunt.

[II.iii]

Enter RICHARDETTO *and* PHILOTIS.

RICHARDETTO. Thou seest, my lovely niece, these
    strange mishaps,
    How all my fortunes turn to my disgrace,
    Wherein I am but as a looker on,
    Whiles others act my shame, and I am silent.

PHILOTIS. But uncle, wherein can this borrowed shape
    Give you content?

RICHARDETTO.   I'll tell thee, gentle niece;
    Thy wanton aunt in her lascivious riots
    Lives now secure, thinks I am surely dead
    In my late journey to Ligorne for you
    (As I have caused it to be rumoured out);
    Now would I see with what an impudence
    She gives scope to her loose adultery,
    And how the common voice allows hereof;
    Thus far I have prevailed.

PHILOTIS.   Alas, I fear
    You mean some strange revenge.

RICHARDETTO.   Oh, be not troubled,
    Your ignorance shall plead for you in all.
    But to our business: what, you learned for certain
    How Signior Florio means to give his daughter
    In marriage to Soranzo?

PHILOTIS.   Yes, for certain.

RICHARDETTO. But how find you young Annabella's love
   Inclined to him?

PHILOTIS.   For aught I could perceive,
   She neither fancies him or any else.

RICHARDETTO.
   There's mystery in that which time must show.
   She used you kindly?

PHILOTIS.   Yes.

RICHARDETTO.   And craved your company?

PHILOTIS. Often.

RICHARDETTO. 'Tis well, it goes as I could wish.
   I am the doctor now, and as for you,
   None knows you; if all fail not, we shall thrive.
   But who comes here?

Enter GRIMALDI.

   I know him, 'tis Grimaldi,
   A Roman and a soldier, near allied
   Unto the Duke of Montferrato; one
   Attending on the Nuncio of the Pope
   That now resides in Parma, by which means
   He hopes to get the love of Annabella.

GRIMALDI. Save you, sir.

RICHARDETTO. And you, sir.

GRIMALDI.   I have heard
   Of your approved skill, which through the city
   Is freely talked of, and would crave your aid.

RICHARDETTO. For what, sir?

GRIMALDI.   Marry, sir, for this –
   But I would speak in private.

RICHARDETTO.   Leave us, cousin.

   Exit PHILOTIS.

GRIMALDI. I love fair Annabella, and would know
   Whether in arts there may not be receipts
   To move affection.

RICHARDETTO.   Sir, perhaps there may,
   But these will nothing profit you.

GRIMALDI.   Not me?

RICHARDETTO. Unless I be mistook, you are a man
   Greatly in favour with the Cardinal.

GRIMALDI. What of that?

RICHARDETTO.   In duty to his Grace,
   I will be bold to tell you, if you seek
   To marry Florio's daughter, you must first
   Remove a bar 'twixt you and her.

GRIMALDI.   Who's that?

RICHARDETTO. Soranzo is the man that hath her heart,
   And while he lives, be sure you cannot speed.

GRIMALDI. Soranzo? What, mine enemy? Is't he?

RICHARDETTO. Is he your enemy?

GRIMALDI.   The man I hate
   Worse than confusion; I'll tell him straight.

RICHARDETTO. Nay, then take mine advice:
   Even for his Grace's sake the Cardinal,
   I'll find a time when he and she do meet,
   Of which I'll give you notice, and to be sure

He shall not scape you, I'll provide a poison
To dip your rapier's point in; if he had
As many heads as Hydra had, he dies.

GRIMALDI. But shall I trust thee, doctor?

RICHARDETTO.   As yourself,
Doubt not in aught. [*Aside.*] Thus shall the fates decree,
By me Soranzo falls, that minèd me.

Exeunt.

[II.iv]

Enter DONADO, BERGETTO, *and* POGGIO.

DONADO. Well, sir, I must be content to be both your
secretary and your messenger myself; I cannot tell what
this letter may work, but as sure as I am alive, if thou
come once to talk with her, I fear thou wilt mar
whatsoever I make.

BERGETTO. You make, uncle? Why, am not I big enough
to carry mine own letter, I pray?

DONADO. Ay, ay, carry a fool's head o'thy own; why, thou
dunce, wouldst thou write a letter, and carry it thyself?

BERGETTO. Yes, that I would, and read it to her with my
own mouth; for you must think, if she will not believe me
myself when she hears me speak, she will not believe
another's handwriting. Oh, you think I am a blockhead,
uncle; no, sir, Poggio knows I have indited a letter myself,
so I have.

POGGIO. Yes, truly, sir, I have it in my pocket.

DONADO. A sweet one, no doubt; pray let's see't.

BERGETTO. I cannot read my own hand very well.
Poggio, read it, Poggio.

DONADO. Begin.

POGGIO *reads*.

POGGIO. Most dainty and honey-sweet mistress, I could
call you fair, and lie as fast as any that loves you, but my
uncle being the elder man, I leave it to him, as more fit
for his age, and the colour of his beard. I am wise
enough to tell you I can board where I see occasion, or if
you like my uncle's wit better than mine, you shall marry
me; if you like mine better than his, I will marry you in
spite of your teeth; so commending my best parts to you,
I rest yours upwards and downwards, or you may choose,
Bergetto.

BERGETTO. Ah ha, here's stuff, uncle.

DONADO. Here's stuff indeed to shame us all;
Pray whose advice did you take in this learned letter?

POGGIO. None, upon my word, but mine own.

BERGETTO. And mine, uncle, believe it, nobody's else;
'twas mine own brain, I thank a good wit for't.

DONADO. Get you home, sir, and look you keep within
doors till I return.

BERGETTO. How? That were a jest indeed; I scorn it,
i'faith.

DONADO. What, you do not?

BERGETTO. Judge me, but I do now.

POGGIO. Indeed, sir, 'tis very unhealthy.

DONADO. Well, sir, if I hear any of your apish running to
motions and fopperies till I come back, you were as good
no; look to't.

Exit DONADO.

BERGETTO. Poggio, shall's steal to see this horse with the
head in's tail?

POGGIO. Ay, but you must take heed of whipping.

BERGETTO. Dost take me for a child, Poggio? Come,
honest Poggio.

Exeunt.

[II.v]

Enter FRIAR *and* GIOVANNI.

FRIAR. Peace. Thou hast told a tale whose every word
Threatens eternal slaughter to the soul.
I'm sorry I have heard it; would mine ears
Had been one minute deaf, before the hour
That thou cam'st to me. O young man cast way,
By the religious number of mine order,
I day and night have waked my aged eyes
Above my strength, to weep on thy behalf;
But Heaven is angry, and be thou resolved,
Thou art a man remarked to taste a mischief.
Look for't; though it come late, it will come sure.

GIOVANNI. Father, in this you are uncharitable;
What I have done, I'll prove both fit and good.
It is a principle which you have taught,
When I was yet your scholar, that the frame

And composition of the mind doth follow
The frame and composition of the body:
So where the body's furniture is beauty,
The mind's must needs be virtue; which allowed,
Virtue itself is reason but refined,
And love, the quintessence of that. This proves
My sister's beauty, being rarely fair,
Is rarely virtuous; chiefly in her love,
And, chiefly in that love, her love to me.
If hers to me, then so is mine to her,
Since in like causes are effects alike.

FRIAR. O ignorance in knowledge! Long ago,
How often have I warned thee this before?
Indeed, if we were sure there were no deity,
Nor Heaven nor Hell, then to be led alone
By nature's light, as were philosophers
Of elder times, might instance some defence.
But 'tis not so; then, madman, thou wilt find
That nature is in Heaven's positions blind.

GIOVANNI. Your age o'errules you; had you youth like mine,
You'd make her love your heaven, and her divine.

FRIAR. Nay then, I see th'art too far sold to hell;
It lies not in the compass of my prayers
To call thee back. Yet let me counsel thee:
Persuade thy sister to some marriage.

GIOVANNI.
Marriage? Why, that's to damn her; that's to prove
Her greedy of variety of lust.

FRIAR. O fearful! If thou wilt not, give me leave
To shrive her, lest she should die unabsolved.

GIOVANNI. At your best leisure, Father; then she'll tell you

How dearly she doth prize my matchless love;
Then you will know what pity 'twere we two
Should have been sundered from each other's arms.
View well her face, and in that little round
You may observe a world of variety;
For colour, lips; for sweet perfumes, her breath;
For jewels, eyes; for threads of purest gold,
Hair; for delicious choice of flowers, cheeks.
Wonder in every portion of that throne!
Hear her but speak, and you will swear the spheres
Make music to the citizens in Heaven;
But Father, what is else for pleasure framed,
Lest I offend your ears, shall go unnamed.

FRIAR. The more I hear, I pity thee the more,
That one so excellent should give those parts
All to a second death. What I can do
Is but to pray; and yet I could advise thee,
Wouldst thou be ruled.

GIOVANNI.   In what?

FRIAR.   Why, leave her yet.
The throne of mercy is above your trespass.
Yet time is left you both –

GIOVANNI.   To embrace each other,
Else let all time be struck quite out of number;
She is like me, and I like her, resolved.

FRIAR. No more, I'll visit her. This grieves me most:
Things being thus, a pair of souls are lost.

Exeunt.

[II.vi]

Enter FLORIO, DONADO, ANNABELLA, *and* PUTANA.

FLORIO. Where's Giovanni?

ANNABELLA.   Newly walked abroad,
And (as I heard him say) gone to the friar,
His reverend tutor.

FLORIO.   That's a blessed man,
A man made up of holiness; I hope
He'll teach him how to gain another world.

DONADO. Fair gentlewoman, here's a letter sent
To you from my young cousin. I dare swear
He loves you in his soul; would you could hear
Sometimes, what I see daily, sighs and tears,
As if his breast were prison to his heart.

FLORIO. Receive it, Annabella.

ANNABELLA.   Alas, good man.

DONADO. What's that she said?

PUTANA. And please you sir, she said 'Alas, good man'.
Truly I do commend him to her every night before her
first sleep, because I would have her dream of him, and
she hearkens to that most religiously.

DONADO. Say'st so? Godamercy, Putana, there's something
for thee, and prithee do what thou canst on his behalf;
sha'not be lost labour, take my word for't.

PUTANA. Thank you most heartily, sir; now I have a
feeling of your mind, let me alone to work.

ANNABELLA. Guardian!

PUTANA. Did you call?

ANNABELLA. Keep this letter.

DONADO. Signior Florio, in any case bid her read it
  instantly.

FLORIO. Keep it for what? Pray read it me here right.

ANNABELLA. I shall, sir.

She reads.

DONADO. How d'ee find her inclined, Signior?

FLORIO. Troth, sir, I know not how; not all so well
  As I could wish.

ANNABELLA. Sir, I am bound to rest your cousin's debtor.
  The jewel I'll return, for if he love,
  I'll count that love a jewel.

DONADO.   Mark you that?
  Nay, keep them both, sweet maid.

ANNABELLA.
  You must excuse me,
  Indeed I will not keep it.

FLORIO.   Where's the ring –
  That which your mother in her will bequeathed,
  And charged you on her blessing not to give't
  To any but your husband? Send back that.

ANNABELLA. I have it not.

FLORIO.   Ha! Have it not? Where is't?

ANNABELLA. My brother in the morning took it from me,
  Said he would wear't today.

FLORIO.   Well, what do you say

To young Bergetto's love? Are you content
To match with him? Speak.

DONADO.   There's the point indeed.

ANNABELLA. What shall I do? I must say something now.

FLORIO. What say? Why d'ee not speak?

ANNABELLA.   Sir, with your leave,
Please you to give me freedom.

FLORIO.   Yes, you have't.

ANNABELLA. Signior Donado, if your nephew mean
To raise his better fortunes in his match,
The hope of me will hinder such a hope;
Sir, if you love him, as I know you do,
Find one more worthy of his choice than me.
In short, I'm sure I sha'not be his wife.

DONADO. Why, here's plain dealing; I commend thee for't,
And all the worst I wish thee, is heaven bless thee!
Your father yet and I will still be friends,
Shall we not, Signior Florio?

FLORIO.   Yes, why not?
Look, here your cousin comes.

Enter BERGETTO *and* POGGIO.

DONADO. Oh coxcomb, what doth he make here?

BERGETTO. Where's my uncle, sirs?

DONADO. What's the news now?

BERGETTO. Save you, uncle, save you; you must not
think I come for nothing, masters, and how is't? What,
you have read my letter? Ah, there I – tickled you,
i'faith.

POGGIO. But 'twere better you had tickled her in another place.

BERGETTO. Sirrah sweetheart, I'll tell thee a good jest, and riddle what 'tis.

ANNABELLA. You say you'd tell me.

BERGETTO. As I was walking just now in the street, I met a swaggering fellow would needs take the wall of me, and because he did thrust me, I very valiantly called him rogue. He hereupon bade me draw; I told him I had more wit than so, but when he saw that I would not, he did so maul me with the hilts of his rapier, that my head sung whilst my feet capered in the kennel.

DONADO. Was ever the like ass seen?

ANNABELLA. And what did you all this while?

BERGETTO. Laugh at him for a gull, till I see the blood run about mine ears, and then I could not choose but find in my heart to cry; till a fellow with a broad beard (they say he is a new-come doctor) called me into his house, and gave me a plaster – look you, here 'tis – and, sir, there was a young wench washed my face and hands most excellently; i'faith I shall love her as long as I live for't. Did she not, Poggio?

POGGIO. Yes, and kissed him, too.

BERGETTO. Why la now, you think I tell a lie, uncle, I warrant.

DONADO. Would he that beat thy blood out of thy head, had beaten some wit into it; for I fear thou never wilt have any.

BERGETTO. Oh, uncle, but there was a wench, would have done a man's heart good to have looked on her; by this light, she had a face, methinks, worth twenty of you, Mistress Annabella.

DONADO. Was ever such a fool born?

ANNABELLA. I am glad she liked you, sir.

BERGETTO. Are you so? By my troth, I thank you, forsooth.

FLORIO. Sure 'twas the doctor's niece, that was last day with us here.

BERGETTO. 'Twas she, 'twas she.

DONADO. How do you know that, simplicity?

BERGETTO. Why, does not he say so? If I should have said no, I should have given him the lie, uncle, and so have deserved a dry beating again; I'll none of that.

FLORIO. A very modest, well-behaved young maid as I have seen.

DONADO. Is she indeed?

FLORIO.   Indeed
She is, if I have any judgement.

DONADO. Well sir, now you are free; you need not care for sending letters now, you are dismissed. Your mistress here will none of you.

BERGETTO. No? Why, what care I for that? I can have wenches enough in Parma for half a crown a piece, cannot I, Poggio?

POGGIO. I'll warrant you, sir.

DONADO. Signior Florio, I thank you for your free recourse you gave for my admittance; and to you, fair maid, that jewel I will give you 'gainst your marriage. Come, will you go, sir?

BERGETTO. Ay, marry will I. Mistress, farewell, mistress, I'll come again tomorrow – farewell, mistress.

Exeunt DONADO, BERGETTO, *and* POGGIO. *Enter* GIOVANNI.

FLORIO. Son, where have you been? What, alone, alone still, still? I would not have it so, you must forsake this ever-bookish humour. Well, your sister hath shook the fool off.

GIOVANNI. 'Twas no match for her.

FLORIO. 'Twas not, indeed; I meant it nothing less. Soranzo is the man I only like. Look on him, Annabella; come, 'tis supper-time, And it grows late.

Exit FLORIO.

GIOVANNI.   Whose jewel's that?

ANNABELLA.   Some sweetheart's.

GIOVANNI. So I think.

ANNABELLA. A lusty youth, Signior Donado, gave it me to wear against my marriage.

GIOVANNI. But you shall not wear it; send it him back again.

ANNABELLA. What, you are jealous?

GIOVANNI. That you shall know anon, at better leisure; Welcome, sweet night, the evening crowns the day.

Exeunt.

maid, that jewel I will give you 'gainst your marriage.
Come, will you go, sir?

BERGETTO. Ay, marry will I. Mistress, farewell, mistress,
I'll come again tomorrow – farewell, mistress.

Exeunt DONADO, BERGETTO, *and* POGGIO. *Enter*
GIOVANNI.

FLORIO. Son, where have you been? What, alone, alone
still, still? I would not have it so, you must forsake this
ever-bookish humour. Well, your sister hath shook the
fool off.

GIOVANNI. 'Twas no match for her.

FLORIO. 'Twas not, indeed; I meant it nothing less.
Soranzo is the man I only like.
Look on him, Annabella; come, 'tis supper-time,
And it grows late.

Exit FLORIO.

GIOVANNI.   Whose jewel's that?

ANNABELLA.   Some sweetheart's.

GIOVANNI. So I think.

ANNABELLA. A lusty youth, Signior Donado, gave it me
to wear against my marriage.

GIOVANNI. But you shall not wear it; send it him back
again.

ANNABELLA. What, you are jealous?

GIOVANNI. That you shall know anon, at better leisure;
Welcome, sweet night, the evening crowns the day.

Exeunt.

this light, she had a face, methinks, worth twenty of you, Mistress Annabella.

DONADO. Was ever such a fool born?

ANNABELLA. I am glad she liked you, sir.

BERGETTO. Are you so? By my troth, I thank you, forsooth.

FLORIO. Sure 'twas the doctor's niece, that was last day with us here.

BERGETTO. 'Twas she, 'twas she.

DONADO. How do you know that, simplicity?

BERGETTO. Why, does not he say so? If I should have said no, I should have given him the lie, uncle, and so have deserved a dry beating again; I'll none of that.

FLORIO. A very modest, well-behaved young maid as I have seen.

DONADO. Is she indeed?

FLORIO.   Indeed
   She is, if I have any judgement.

DONADO. Well sir, now you are free; you need not care for sending letters now, you are dismissed. Your mistress here will none of you.

BERGETTO. No? Why, what care I for that? I can have wenches enough in Parma for half a crown a piece, cannot I, Poggio?

POGGIO. I'll warrant you, sir.

DONADO. Signior Florio, I thank you for your free recourse you gave for my admittance; and to you, fair

POGGIO. Lose no time, then.

BERGETTO. I will beget a race of wise men and
  constables, that shall cart whores at their own charges,
  and break the Duke's peace, ere I have done myself.
  Come away.

Exeunt.

[III.ii]

Enter FLORIO, GIOVANNI, SORANZO, ANNABELLA,
PUTANA *and* VASQUES.

FLORIO. My lord Soranzo, though I must confess
  The proffers that are made me have been great
  In marriage of my daughter, yet the hope
  Of your still rising honours have prevailed
  Above all other jointures. Here she is.
  She knows my mind; speak for yourself to her,
  And hear you, daughter, see you use him nobly.
  For any private speech I'll give you time.
  Come, son, and you the rest, let them alone,
  Agree they as they may.

SORANZO.   I thank you, sir.

GIOVANNI. Sister, be not all woman, think on me.

SORANZO. Vasques?

VASQUES. My lord.

SORANZO. Attend me without.

Exeunt all except SORANZO *and* ANNABELLA.

[III.i]

Enter BERGETTO *and* POGGIO.

BERGETTO. Does my uncle think to make me a baby still? No, Poggio, he shall know I have a sconce now.

POGGIO. Ay, let him not bob you off like an ape with an apple.

BERGETTO. 'Sfoot, I will have the wench, if he were ten uncles, in despite of his nose, Poggio.

POGGIO. Hold him to the grindstone, and give not a jot of ground; she hath in a manner promised you already.

BERGETTO. True, Poggio, and her uncle the doctor swore I should marry her.

POGGIO. He swore, I remember.

BERGETTO. And I will have her, that's more; didst see the codpiece-point she gave me, and the box of marmalade?

POGGIO. Very well; and kissed you, that my chops watered at the sight on't; there's no way but to clap up a marriage in hugger-mugger.

BERGETTO. I will do't; for I tell thee, Poggio, I begin to grow valiant, methinks, and my courage begins to rise.

POGGIO. Should you be afraid of your uncle?

BERGETTO. Hang him, old doting rascal! No, I say I will have her.

ANNABELLA. Sir, what's your will with me?

SORANZO.   Do you not know
What I should tell you?

ANNABELLA.   Yes, you'll say you love me.

SORANZO. And I'll swear it too; will you believe it?

ANNABELLA. 'Tis no point of faith.

Enter GIOVANNI *above.*

SORANZO.   Have you not will to love?

ANNABELLA. Not you.

SORANZO. Whom then?

ANNABELLA.   That's as the fates infer.

GIOVANNI. Of those I'm regent now.

SORANZO.   What mean you, sweet?

ANNABELLA. To live and die a maid.

SORANZO.   Oh that's unfit.

GIOVANNI. Here's one can say that's but a woman's note.

SORANZO. Did you but see my heart, then would you
swear –

ANNABELLA. That you were dead.

GIOVANNI.   That's true, or somewhat near it.

SORANZO. See you these true love's tears?

ANNABELLA.   No.

GIOVANNI.   Now she winks.

SORANZO. They plead to you for grace.

ANNABELLA.   Yet nothing speak.

SORANZO. Oh grant my suit.

ANNABELLA.   What is't?

SORANZO.   To let me live.

ANNABELLA. Take it –

SORANZO.   Still yours.

ANNABELLA.   That is not mine to give.

GIOVANNI. One such another word would kill his hopes.

SORANZO. Mistress, to leave those fruitless strifes of wit,
    Know I have loved you long, and loved you truly;
    Not hope of what you have, but what you are
    Hath drawn me on; then let me not in vain
    Still feel the rigour of your chaste disdain.
    I'm sick, and sick to th'heart.

ANNABELLA. Help, aqua vitae!

SORANZO.What mean you?

ANNABELLA.Why, I thought you had been sick.

SORANZO. Do you mock my love?

GIOVANNI. There, sir, she was too nimble.

SORANZO. 'Tis plain; she laughs at me. These scornful
    taunts neither become your modesty, or years.

ANNABELLA.You are no looking-glass, or if you were, I'd
    dress my language by you.

GIOVANNI. I'm confirmed.

ANNABELLA.To put you out of doubt, my lord, methinks
    your common sense should make you understand that if

I loved you, or desired your love, some way I should have
given you better taste; but since you are a nobleman, and
one I would not wish should spend his youth in hopes, let
me advise you here to forbear your suit, and think I wish
you well, I tell you this.

SORANZO. Is't you speak this?

ANNABELLA.   Yes, I myself; yet know –
Thus far I give you comfort – if mine eyes
Could have picked out a man amongst all those
That sued to me, to make a husband of,
You should have been that man; let this suffice.
Be noble in your secrecy, and wise.

GIOVANNI. Why now I see she loves me.

ANNABELLA.   One word more:
As ever virtue lived within your mind,
As ever noble courses were your guide,
As ever you would have me know you loved me,
Let not my father know hereof by you;
If I hereafter find that I must marry,
It shall be you or none.

SORANZO.   I take that promise.

ANNABELLA. Oh, oh, my head.

SORANZO.   What's the matter? Not well?

ANNABELLA. Oh, I begin to sicken.

GIOVANNI.   Heaven forbid.

Exit from above.

SORANZO. Help, help, within there ho. Look to your
daughter, Signior Florio!

Enter FLORIO, GIOVANNI, *and* PUTANA.

FLORIO. Hold her up, she swoons.

GIOVANNI. Sister, how d'ee?

ANNABELLA.   Sick; brother, are you there?

FLORIO. Convey her to her bed instantly, whilst I send for
a physician; quickly, I say.

PUTANA. Alas, poor child.

Exeunt all except SORANZO. *Enter* VASQUES.

VASQUES. My lord.

SORANZO. Oh Vasques, now I doubly am undone,
Both in my present and my future hopes:
She plainly told me that she could not love,
And thereupon soon sickened, and I fear
Her life's in danger.

VASQUES. By'r lady, sir, and so is yours, if you knew all. –
'Las, sir, I am sorry for that; maybe 'tis but the maid's
sickness, an overflux of youth, and then, sir, there is no
such present remedy as present marriage. But hath she
given you an absolute denial?

SORANZO. She hath and she hath not; I'm full of grief,
But what she said, I'll tell thee as we go.

Exeunt.

[III.iii]

Enter GIOVANNI *and* PUTANA.

PUTANA. Oh sir, we are all undone, quite undone, utterly
    undone, and shamed forever; your sister, oh, your sister.

GIOVANNI. What of her? For heaven's sake speak: how
    does she?

PUTANA. Oh that ever I was born to see this day.

GIOVANNI. She is not dead, ha, is she?

PUTANA. Dead? No, she is quick; 'tis worse, she is with
    child. You know what you have done; Heaven forgive 'ee.
    'Tis too late to repent now, Heaven help us.

GIOVANNI. With child? How dost thou know't?

PUTANA. How do I know't? Am I, at these years, ignorant
    what the meanings of qualms and waterpangs be? Of
    changing of colours, queasiness of stomachs, pukings, and
    another thing that I could name? Do not, for her and
    your credit's sake, spend the time in asking how, and
    which way, 'tis so; she is quick, upon my word; if you let
    a physician see her water, y'are undone.

GIOVANNI. But in what case is she?

PUTANA. Prettily amended; 'twas but a fit which I soon
    espied, and she must look for often henceforward.

GIOVANNI. Commend me to her, bid her take no care;
    Let not the doctor visit her, I charge you;
    Make some excuse till I return. Oh me,
    I have a world of business in my head.
    Do not discomfort her; how does this news perplex me!
    If my father come to her, tell him she's recovered well;

Say 'twas but some ill diet. D'ee hear, woman?
Look you to't.

PUTANA. I will, sir.

Exeunt.

(III.iv)

Enter FLORIO *and* RICHARDETTO.

FLORIO. And how d'ee find her, sir?

RICHARDETTO.   Indifferent well;
I see no danger, scarce perceive she's sick,
But that she told me she had lately eaten
Melons, and, as she thought, those disagreed
With her young stomach.

FLORIO.   Did you give her aught?

RICHARDETTO. An easy surfeit water, nothing else.
You need not doubt her health; I rather think
Her sickness is a fullness of her blood.
You understand me?

FLORIO.   I do; you counsel well,
And once within these few days will so order't
She shall be married ere she know the time.

RICHARDETTO. Yet let not haste, sir, make unworthy
choice;
That were dishonour.

FLORIO.   Master doctor, no;
I will not do so neither. In plain words,
My lord Soranzo is the man I mean.

RICHARDETTO. A noble and a virtuous gentleman.

FLORIO. As any is in Parma. Not far hence
  Dwells Father Bonaventure, a grave friar,
  Once tutor to my son; now at his cell
  I'll have 'em married.

RICHARDETTO. You have plotted wisely.

FLORIO.   I'll send one straight
  To speak with him tonight.

RICHARDETTO. Soranzo's wise, he will delay no time.

FLORIO. It shall be so.

  Enter FRIAR *and* GIOVANNI.

FRIAR.   Good peace be here, and love.

FLORIO. Welcome, religious friar; you are one
  That still bring blessing to the place you come to.

GIOVANNI. Sir, with what speed I could, I did my best
  To draw this holy man from forth his cell
  To visit my sick sister, that with words
  Of ghostly comfort in this time of need
  He might absolve her, whether she live or die.

FLORIO. 'Twas well done, Giovanni; thou herein
  Hast showed a Christian's care, a brother's love.
  Come, Father, I'll conduct you to her chamber,
  And one thing would entreat you.

FRIAR.   Say on, sir.

FLORIO.
  I have a father's dear impression,
  And wish before I fall into my grave,
  That I might see her married, as 'tis fit;

A word from you, grave man, will win her more
Than all our best persuasions.

FRIAR.   Gentle sir,
All this I'll say, that Heaven may prosper her.

Exeunt.

(III.v)

Enter GRIMALDI.

GRIMALDI. Now if the doctor keep his word, Soranzo,
    Twenty to one you miss your bride! I know
    'Tis an unnoble act, and not becomes
    A soldier's valour; but in terms of love,
    Where merit cannot sway, policy must.
    I am resolved; if this physician
    Play not on both hands, then Soranzo falls.

Enter RICHARDETTO.

RICHARDETTO.
    You are come as I could wish; this very night
    Soranzo, 'tis ordained, must be affied
    To Annabella; and for aught I know,
    Married.

GRIMALDI. How!

RICHARDETTO. Yet your patience.
    The place, 'tis Friar Bonaventure's cell.
    Now I would wish you to bestow this night
    In watching thereabouts; 'tis but a night.
    If you miss now, tomorrow I'll know all.

GRIMALDI. Have you the poison?

RICHARDETTO.   Here 'tis, in this box.
  Doubt nothing, this will do't; in any case,
  As you respect your life, be quick and sure.

GRIMALDI. I'll speed him.

RICHARDETTO.   Do; away, for 'tis not safe
  You should be seen much here – ever my love.

GRIMALDI. And mine to you.

  Exit GRIMALDI.

RICHARDETTO. So, if this hit, I'll laugh and hug revenge;
  And they that now dream of a wedding-feast
  May chance to mourn the lusty bridegroom's ruin.
  But to my other business: niece Philotis!

  Enter PHILOTIS.

PHILOTIS. Uncle?

RICHARDETTO. My lovely niece, you have bethought 'ee?

PHILOTIS.Yes, and as you counselled,
  Fashioned my heart to love him; but he swears
  He will tonight be married; for he fears
  His uncle else, if he should know the drift,
  Will hinder all, and call his coz to shrift.

RICHARDETTO. Tonight? Why, best of all; but let me see,
  I – ha – yes, – so it shall be: in disguise
  We'll early to the friar's. I have thought on't.

  Enter BERGETTO *and* POGGIO.

PHILOTIS. Uncle, he comes.

RICHARDETTO.   Welcome, my worthy coz.

BERGETTO. Lass, pretty lass, come, buss, lass. Ah ha, Poggio!

POGGIO. There's hope of this yet.

RICHARDETTO.You shall have time enough. Withdraw a little. We must confer at large.

BERGETTO. Have you not sweetmeats or dainty devices for me?

PHILOTIS.You shall have enough, sweetheart.

BERGETTO. 'Sweetheart'! Mark that, Poggio; by my troth I cannot choose but kiss thee once more for that word sweetheart. Poggio, I have a monstrous swelling about my stomach, whatsoever the matter be.

POGGIO. You shall have physic for't, sir.

RICHARDETTO. Time runs apace.

BERGETTO. Time's a blockhead.

RICHARDETTO.
Be ruled; when we have done what's fit to do,
Then you may kiss your fill, and bed her too.

Exeunt.

(III.vi)

Enter the FRIAR in his study, sitting in a chair; ANNABELLA kneeling and whispering to him, a table before them and wax-lights; she weeps, and wrings her hands.

FRIAR. I am glad to see this penance; for, believe me,
You have unripped a soul so foul and guilty

As I must tell you true, I marvel how
The earth hath borne you up; but weep, weep on,
These tears may do you good; weep faster yet,
Whiles I do read a lecture.

ANNABELLA.   Wretched creature.

FRIAR. Ay, you are wretched, miserably wretched,
Almost condemned alive. There is a place –
List, daughter – in a black and hollow vault,
Where day is never seen. There shines no sun,
But flaming horror of consuming fires –
A lightless sulphur, choked with smoky fogs,
Of an infected darkness. In this place
Dwell many thousand, thousand sundry sorts
Of never-dying deaths: there damned souls
Roar without pity; there are gluttons fed
With toads and adders; there is burning oil
Poured down the drunkard's throat; the usurer
Is forced to sup whole draughts of molten gold;
There is the murderer forever stabbed,
Yet can he never die; there lies the wanton
On racks of burning steel, whiles in his soul
He feels the torment of his raging lust.

ANNABELLA. Mercy, oh mercy.

FRIAR.   There stand these wretched things
Who have dreamed out whole years in lawless sheets
And secret incests, cursing one another;
Then you will wish each kiss your brother gave
Had been a dagger's point; then you shall hear
How he will cry, 'Oh, would my wicked sister
Had first been damn'd when she did yield to lust!'
But soft, methinks I see repentance work
New motions in your heart; say, how is't with you?

ANNABELLA. Is there no way left to redeem my miseries?

FRIAR. There is, despair not; Heaven is merciful,
  And offers grace even now. 'Tis thus agreed:
  First, for your honour's safety, that you marry
  The lord Soranzo; next, to save your soul,
  Leave off this life, and henceforth live to him.

ANNABELLA. Ay me.

FRIAR.   Sigh not. I know the baits of sin
  Are hard to leave; oh, 'tis a death to do't.
  Remember what must come; are you content?

ANNABELLA. I am.

FRIAR.   I like it well; we'll take the time.
  Who's near us there?

  Enter FLORIO *and* GIOVANNI.

FLORIO.   Did you call, Father?

FRIAR. Is Lord Soranzo come?

FLORIO.   He stays below.

FRIAR. Have you acquainted him at full?

FLORIO.   I have,
  And he is overjoyed.

FRIAR.   And so are we.
  Bid him come near.

GIOVANNI.   My sister weeping, ha?
  I fear this friar's falsehood. I will call him.
  Exit.

FLORIO. Daughter, are you resolved?

ANNABELLA.   Father, I am.

Enter GIOVANNI, SORANZO, *and* VASQUES.

FLORIO. My lord Soranzo, here:
  Give me your hand. For that, I give you this.

SORANZO. Lady, say you so too?

ANNABELLA.   I do, and vow
  To live with you and yours.

FRIAR. Timely resolved.
  My blessing rest on both; more to be done,
  You may perform it in the morning sun.

  Exeunt.

(III.vii)

Enter GRIMALDI *with his rapier drawn, and a dark-lantern.*

GRIMALDI. 'Tis early night as yet, and yet too soon
  To finish such a work; here I will lie
  To listen who comes next.

  He lies down. Enter BERGETTO *and* PHILOTIS *disguised,
  and after* RICHARDETTO *and* POGGIO.

BERGETTO. We are almost at the place, I hope, sweetheart.

GRIMALDI. I hear them near, and heard one say 'sweetheart';
  'Tis he; now guide my hand, some angry Justice,
  Home to his bosom! Now have at you, sir.

  Strikes BERGETTO *and exits.*

BERGETTO. Oh help, help, here's a stitch fallen in my
  guts. Oh, for a flesh-tailor quickly – Poggio!

PHILOTIS. What ails my love?

BERGETTO. I am sure I cannot piss forward and
backward, and yet I am wet before and behind. Lights,
lights, ho lights!

PHILOTIS. Alas, some villain here has slain my love.

RICHARDETTO. Oh Heaven forbid it; raise up the next
neighbours instantly, Poggio, and bring lights.

Exit POGGIO.

How is't, Bergetto? Slain? It cannot be; are you sure
y'are hurt?

BERGETTO. Oh, my belly seethes like a porridge-pot;
some cold water, I shall boil over else; my whole body is
in a sweat, that you may wring my shirt; feel here – why,
Poggio.

Enter POGGIO *with* OFFICERS, *and lights and halberds.*

POGGIO. Here; alas, how do you?

RICHARDETTO.
Give me a light. What's here? All blood! O sirs,
Signior Donado's nephew now is slain!
Follow the murderer with all the haste
Up to the city; he cannot be far hence.
Follow, I beseech you.

OFFICERS. Follow, follow, follow!

Exeunt OFFICERS.

RICHARDETTO. Tear off thy linen, coz, to stop his wounds.
Be of good comfort, man.

BERGETTO. Is all this mine own blood? Nay then, good-

night with me. Poggio, commend me to my uncle, dost
hear? Bid him for my sake make much of this wench –
oh, I am going the wrong way sure, my belly aches so –
oh, farewell, Poggio, – oh – oh –

Dies.

PHILOTIS. Oh, he is dead.

POGGIO.   How! Dead!

RICHARDETTO.   He's dead indeed.
  'Tis now too late to weep; let's have him home,
  And with what speed we may, find out the murderer.

POGGIO. Oh my master, my master, my master.

Exeunt.

[III.viii]

Enter VASQUES *and* HIPPOLITA.

HIPPOLITA. Betrothed?

VASQUES.   I saw it.

HIPPOLITA.   And when's the marriage-day?

VASQUES. Some two days hence.

HIPPOLITA. Two days? Why, man, I would but wish two
  hours
  To send him to his last, and lasting sleep.
  And, Vasques, thou shalt see I'll do it bravely.

VASQUES. I do not doubt your wisdom, nor (I trust) you
  my secrecy; I am infinitely yours.

HIPPOLITA. I will be thine in spite of my disgrace.
　　So soon? O wicked man! I durst be sworn
　　He'd laugh to see me weep.

VASQUES. And that's a villainous fault in him.

HIPPOLITA. No, let him laugh; I'm armed in my resolves.
　　Be thou still true.

VASQUES. I should get little by treachery against so
　　hopeful a preferment as I am like to climb to.

HIPPOLITA. Even to my bosom, Vasques. Let my youth
　　Revel in these new pleasures; if we thrive,
　　He now hath but a pair of days to live.

　　Exeunt.

(III.ix)

Enter FLORIO, DONADO, RICHARDETTO, POGGIO
and OFFICERS.

FLORIO. 'Tis bootless now to show yourself a child,
　　Signior Donado; what is done, is done;
　　Spend not the time in tears, but seek for justice.

RICHARDETTO. I must confess, somewhat I was in fault,
　　That had not first acquainted you what love
　　Passed 'twixt him and my niece; but, as I live,
　　His fortune grieves me as it were mine own.

DONADO. Alas, poor creature, he meant no man harm,
　　That I am sure of.

FLORIO.　　　　　I believe that too;
　　But stay, my masters, are you sure you saw
　　The murderer pass here?

OFFICER. And it please you, sir, we are sure we saw a
    ruffian, with a naked weapon in his hand all bloody, get
    into my Lord Cardinal's Grace's gate, that we are sure of;
    but for fear of his Grace (bless us) we durst go no further.

DONADO. Know you what manner of man he was?

OFFICER. Yes, sure, I know the man; they say he is a
    soldier – he that loved your daughter, sir, an't please ye;
    'twas he for certain.

FLORIO. Grimaldi, on my life.

OFFICER. Ay, ay, the same.

RICHARDETTO. The Cardinal is noble; he no doubt
    Will give true justice.

DONADO.   Knock some one at the gate.

POGGIO. I'll knock, sir.

    POGGIO *knocks*.

SERVANT [*within*]. What would'ee?

FLORIO. We require speech with the Lord Cardinal
    About some present business; pray inform
    His Grace that we are here.

    Enter CARDINAL *and* GRIMALDI.

CARDINAL. Why, how now, friends? What saucy mates are
    you
    That know nor duty nor civility?
    Are we a person fit to be your host?
    Or is our house become your common inn
    To beat our doors at pleasure? What such haste
    Is yours as that it cannot wait fit times?
    Are you the masters of this commonwealth,
    And know no more discretion? Oh, your news

Is here before you: you have lost a nephew
Donado, last night by Grimaldi slain;
Is that your business? Well, sir, we have knowledge on't;
Let that suffice.

GRIMALDI.   In presence of your Grace,
In thought I never meant Bergetto harm.
But, Florio, you can tell with how much scorn
Soranzo, backed with his confederates,
Hath often wronged me; I, to be revenged
(For that I could not win him else to fight),
Had thought by way of ambush to have killed him,
But was unluckily therein mistook;
Else he had felt what late Bergetto did.
And though my fault to him were merely chance,
Yet humbly I submit me to your Grace,
To do with me as you please.

CARDINAL.   Rise up, Grimaldi.
You citizens of Parma, if you seek
For justice, know, as Nuncio from the Pope,
For this offence I here receive Grimaldi
Into his holiness' protection.
He is no common man, but nobly born,
Of princes' blood, though you, Sir Florio,
Thought him too mean a husband for your daughter.
If more you seek for, you must go to Rome,
For he shall thither; learn more wit, for shame.
Bury your dead – away, Grimaldi, leave 'em.

Exeunt CARDINAL *and* GRIMALDI.

DONADO. Is this a churchman's voice? Dwells justice here?

FLORIO. Justice is fled to Heaven and comes no nearer.
Soranzo; was't for him? O impudence!
Had he the face to speak it, and not blush?